Published in 2018 by **The Rosen Publishing Group, Inc.**
29 East 21st Street, New York, NY 10010

Cataloging-in-Publication Data

Names: Yates, Jane.
Title: I can draw unicorns / Jane Yates.
Description: New York : PowerKids Press, 2018. | Series: I can draw!: mythical creatures | Includes index.
Identifiers: LCCN ISBN 9781538323526 (pbk.) | ISBN 9781538322567 (library bound) | ISBN 9781538323533 (6 pack)
Subjects: LCSH: Unicorns in art--Juvenile literature. | Animals, Mythical, in art--Juvenile literature. |
   Drawing--Technique--Juvenile literature.
Classification: LCC NC825.M9 Y38 2018 | DDC 743'.87--dc23

Developed and produced for Rosen by BlueApple*Works* Inc.

Creative Director: Melissa McClellan
Managing Editor for BlueApple*Works*: Melissa McClellan
Designer: T.J. Choleva
Photo Research: Jane Reid
Editor: Janice Dyer

Illustrations and Photo Credits: cover background szefei/Shutterstock; cover bottom right Pushkin/Shutterstock; cover center Helen Lane/Shutterstock; cover top left Nancy White/Shutterstock; cover top right Simon Streatfeild; title page. p. 6, 7, top half 8, 10, 11 Simon Streatfeild; TOC, p. 4 Lotus_studio/Shutterstock; p. 4 right Melkor3D /Shutterstock; p. 5 left, p. 5 middle Austen Photography; p. 5 left bottom domnitsky/Shutterstock; p. 5 bottom right Fotana/Shutterstock; p. 5 top right Coprid/Shutterstock; p. 5 top middle PhuShutter/Shutterstock; p. 8 bottom, 9 jen_art /Shutterstock; p. 11 top right oksanika/Shutterstock; p. 13 middle right aekikuis/Shutterstock; Janet Kompare-Fritz p. 14–15, background image szefei/Shutterstock; Simon Streatfeild p.16–17, background image Oliver Denker/Shutterstock; Simon Streatfeild p.18–19, background image Rashevska Nataliia/Shutterstock; Simon Streatfeild p.22–23, background image Unholy Vault Designs/Shutterstock; Simon Streatfeild p.26–27, background image NextMars/Shutterstock; Simon Streatfeild p.30–31, background image NextMars/Shutterstock; Joshua Avramson; p. 20–21 final colored art, p. 21, Nancy White/Shutterstock, background image Standret/Shutterstock; Joshua Avramson; p. 24–25 final colored art, p. 25, Helen Lane/Shutterstock, background image Unholy Vault Designs/Shutterstock; Joshua Avramson; p. 28–29 final colored art, p. 29, Pushkin/Shutterstock, background image NextMars/Shutterstock

Manufactured in the United States of America
CPSIA Compliance Information: Batch BW18PK: For Further Information contact Rosen Publishing, New York, New York at 1-800-237-9932.

CONTENTS

UNICORNS IN THE MYTHS

A unicorn is a mythical beast known for having a long, spiralled horn that comes out of its forehead. The first known reports of unicorns came from natural histories written in Ancient Greece. These reports claimed that the creatures lived in India. These ancient texts describe a number of different types of unicorns. All of them had four legs, hooves, and a horn, but some were said to look like horses, while others looked more like goats or donkeys. It was believed that their horns had healing properties. Unicorns are one of the only mythical creatures that are not based on human fears. Unicorns are not scary monsters. Instead, they're admired and respected. They're thought to be animals of pure good. Because of this, some myths have said they could only be captured by a girl or young woman with a true, generous heart.

In most modern stories, all unicorns are described in a similar way. Their fur is usually pure white, or a similar light pastel color. They tend to look like horses and are usually exceptionally beautiful. Their horns can be short or long, but they usually have a spiral pattern. That said, just because unicorns are usually shown this way today doesn't mean you have to draw your unicorn in the same way. Feel free to add new features and try different colors!

GET READY TO DRAW

Part of the fun of drawing is the huge variety of materials and techniques you can use. However, when you're getting started, it's usually best to start simple. Beginning artists have used pencils, pens, and paper for generations. If you have an art supply store near you, the staff there can usually recommend good starting equipment. They might even have starter kits you can buy. One invaluable piece of equipment is a sketchbook, a big book filled with blank pages. You can fill a sketchbook with practice drawings, and it can be fun to go back and see how you've improved.

Once you get the basics of putting pencil to paper, you'll want to start inking your drawings. Inking is when you go over the initial pencil marks with pen, which can help give your drawings a more finished, look. Another piece of equipment that many artists begin using more once they get a little better is the eraser. Unlike the eraser at the end of your pencil, artists' erasers come in a variety of shapes and have a variety of uses. Some are just for getting rid of mistakes, while others help with advanced techniques like shading.

The core of a pencil is made of graphite, which is what makes a mark. Drawing pencils come in sets with different levels of graphite hardness. The softer the graphite, the darker a mark it makes.

There are tons of different types of drawing paper, and they all have different purposes. Tracing paper is very light, and is great for copying examples to see how to draw them.

Pens, like pencils, also come in different thicknesses. You can buy them in sets, and different sets might be recommended for different styles of drawing.

Different coloring tools have different feels, and it will take some **experimentation** to figure out what you like best. Colored pens, pencils, and markers are all great places to start.

CARTOON STYLE DRAWING

Cartooning is a style many artists start out with. Because cartoons don't need to be realistic, it can be an easier style to get started with. With cartoons, an artist can provide a lot of information with just a few simple lines. A great place to begin is drawing faces of humans or animals. It's amazing how much can be shown through facial expressions! First, draw an oval to represent the head. Then, mark a cross, or t-shape, in the middle of the oval. This cross will help guide where to place facial features like the eyes, a nose, and a mouth.

Draw an oval (or egg).

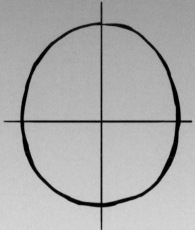

Divide the oval into four sections with a crossed lines.

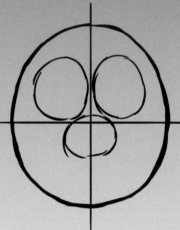

Draw three more ovals — two upright for the eyes, and one on its side for the nose.

Draw two more ovals or circles for pupils and a curved line for the mouth. A line curved up is a smile. A line curved down is a frown.

Erase the cross and fill in the pupils. Add a few lines for hair, too.

Two more ovals work well for ears, and a few dots for freckles help give your cartoon some personality.

Once you know the basics of drawing a face, you can start experimenting. You can keep your cartoons simple, or you can make them more complex. Eyes can be two dots, or they can be huge, expressive shapes. You can use simple lines for mouths and eyebrows, but their placement can show a wide variety of emotions. You can also exaggerate them with different shapes, sizes, and **textures**. A nose might just be a curved line, or it might be so big you can count individual nose hairs. There's no one right way to draw cartoons.

Eyebrows can show a huge variety of emotions.

Are they big, fuzzy, and out of control?

Or are they slim and shocked?

Even simple lines can add a lot to your drawings!

Once you know how to draw a face, it's time to think about other features. How does your character wear their hair? Whatever their style, remember, you don't have to worry about every little hair. You can draw an outline, and people will understand. You can also fill in the outline with a few line strokes to give the appearance of texture. You can use these same techniques for facial hair like beards and mustaches. A few dots can give the appearance of rugged **stubble**. You can use these same techniques to draw animal features.

If you were a hairstylist, what look would best suit your character? Maybe some wild curls?

Or maybe your character has gone bald. What might that say about their personality?

Long, floppy hair can give a laid-back impression.

Spiky hair goes everywhere!

CARTOON STYLE BODY SHAPE

When you begin drawing cartoon bodies, it's best to work with basic shapes. Simplicity is key. A popular shape that many artists use for bodies is a pear shape. One thing to remember is to try to avoid straight lines. These can look **static** and **lifeless**. Cartoons are supposed to be fun, and curvy, round bodies can give a feeling of playfulness.

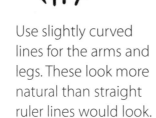

Start with an oval for the head, and put it on top of a pear shape. Don't forget two circles for eyes.

Use slightly curved lines for the arms and legs. These look more natural than straight ruler lines would look.

Add some smoothed ovals for the hands and feet. Connect your head to your body with a neck before the head can float away!

On top of this, you can add clothes and other details like hair.

Good shapes to use when drawing animals are ovals, circles, and rounded rectangles. Try mixing and matching the shapes to best fit your character's outline.

A long oval shape

Circles and overlapping circles

A rectangle with rounded corners

Use circles and overlapping circles to outline the body shape of animals.

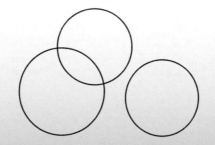

REALISTIC STYLE DRAWING

You can start drawing more realistic looking animals using the same shapes and forms as you do with cartoon characters. However, now that you know how to define the forms, it will help if you outline a simple skeleton structure using lines. They will guide you in relation to the animal's joints, such as those in its legs, in order to draw it in the position you want.

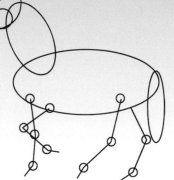

Use rounded shapes to outline the head and body of your character like you did before. Don't worry if it looks a little rough, you can always clean it up!

Now add some lines that are connected with circles where the joints would be for the legs.

Next, outline the body and legs using the skeleton as a guide.

Finally, add details such as the hoofs, mane, and tail.

Use circle shapes and curved lines to outline the position for the cheek and the **muzzle**.

MANGA STYLE DRAWING

There are countless styles that a new artist can explore. From cartoons to photorealism, it's all a matter of what you enjoy drawing and looking at. One style that has proven extremely popular is manga. Manga started out as a style of Japanese comics, but today its popularity has spread all over the world. Some popular examples of manga include Sailor Moon and Dragon Ball Z. Animated cartoons that are based on manga are called anime.

Characters in manga are famous for having large eyes that can express a lot. In contrast, most of their other facial features are usually pretty simple. However, they tend to make up for this simplicity with their big, crazy hairstyles! Most manga characters have a few similarities, but like other styles of art, each artist has their own way of doing things. You can use manga style drawing for humans or for animals.

MANGA STYLE EYES

In manga, eyes are one of the most noticeable features. They tend to be large, and can show a variety of emotions.

MANGA STYLE HAIR

Manga-style hair is also immediately recognizable. It's often spiky and wild, and totally impossible to pull off in real life!

First, make a general outline of your character's hair. Then add some strands in different sizes and shapes.

Usually hair all flows out from a single point on the top of the head, but you might want to experiment with different approaches.

MANGA STYLE BODIES

Manga bodies tend to be more realistic than cartoons. Start with an oval for the head and rectangles for the body. For limbs, you can use the skeleton techniques you learned on page 9. Look at other examples of manga for inspiration for manga style poses.

Start by using general shapes for your head and body, with jointed lines for limbs.

Then, outline the rest of your character. Once it's done, go over the outline in a thicker pencil, and erase your guidelines. Now you can color it in!

You can apply these same techniques to drawing animals, but you'll probably use different shapes to build their bodies.

FINISHING YOUR DRAWINGS—INKING

Once you're done drawing, erase all your guidelines and everything else you don't want in the final version. You can erase these lines one step at a time as you go, or all at once at the end. You can also go over your drawing in pencil again to make the lines bolder. Once you're done with a pencil drawing, you can also go over your lines with a pen. This process is called inking.

Complete your drawing.

Erase all extra lines that you used to create your character.

Go over your drawing again with a thicker pencil, or with an inking pen.

COLORING YOUR DRAWINGS

Most art looks just fine in black and white. However, many artists believe that color is the only way to really get their art to pop! If you feel the same way, there are a variety of tools and techniques you can use to achieve your desired effect. Pencils, crayons, and markers are great to get a feel for how coloring works. As you get better you might even want to try watercolor paints!

COLORING WITH PENCILS OR CRAYONS

Shading is a technique that helps create contrast between light and dark areas. First, figure out where your drawing's light source is. Is it above your character? Below it? This will help you to determine what is in shadow, and what is brightly lit. Well-lit areas will usually be brighter, while shadowy areas will be darker.

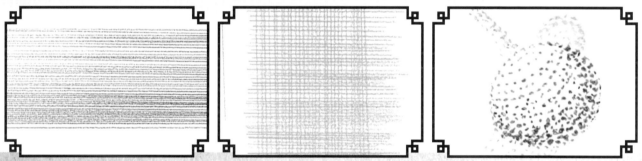

Hatching is a shading technique that uses lines that all go in the same direction.

Cross-hatching is just like hatching except you also add lines going in an opposite direction. This creates a richer texture in drawings.

Stippling is another shading technique, but instead of using lines, it uses dots. The more dots, the more shaded your subject looks.

COLORING WITH MARKERS

Markers are a great tool to use for coloring. They're simple, they don't need to be prepared in any way for use, and once the color is on the page, it dries fairly quickly. Because marker ink is liquid, it creates a smoother mark than pencils or crayons do.

Choose the colors you want to work with.

Fill in each separate section of your drawing, just like in a coloring book.

You can shade your drawing by using darker or lighter markers.

COLORING WITH WATERCOLORS

Watercolor paints come in tubes, or you can get multiple colors in a pan. The nice thing about using a pan is that you can remove the clear lid and use it as a watercolor palette. You can use the palette to mix together different colors to create new ones.

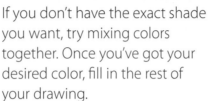

Choose the sections of your drawing you want to fill in with paint.

If you don't have the exact shade you want, try mixing colors together. Once you've got your desired color, fill in the rest of your drawing.

If you accidentally cover up some of your lines with paint, don't worry! Just wait for the paint to dry, and then go over the line again with pencil.

WORKING WITH COLORS

A color wheel is a tool that artists use to help understand colors. It shows what colors look like mixed together, and helps to give an idea of how different colors are related. It also shows which colors look good together, and which ones don't.

There are three types of colors on a color wheel: primary colors, secondary colors, and tertiary colors. Primary colors are blue, red, and yellow. These colors can't be made by mixing other colors together. Secondary colors are green, orange, and violet or purple. These colors can be made by mixing two primary colors together. For example, red and blue together make violet. Tertiary colors are made by mixing a primary color with a secondary color that's beside it on the color wheel.

P – Primary colors
S – Secondary colors
T – Tertiary colors

Yellow and blue are two neighboring primary colors. Mixing them together will create the secondary color green.

Blue and green are two neighboring primary and secondary colors. Mixing them together will create the blue-green tertiary color.

COMPLEMENTARY COLORS

Colors that are located directly opposite from each other on the color wheel are considered complementary colors. That means they balance each other out. Primary colors are complemented by secondary colors. For example, orange complements blue, green complements red, and violet complements yellow. Using these colors together in a drawing can help create great looking art!

GOOFY UNICORN

1 Start with an oval shape for the head. Add two triangular shapes for the ears, then add a long pointy shape for the horn.

2 Add another oval shape to outline the unicorn's muzzle.

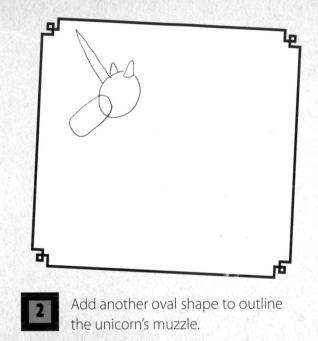

3 Add another long oval for the neck.

4 Form the body shape with two more overlapping oval shapes.

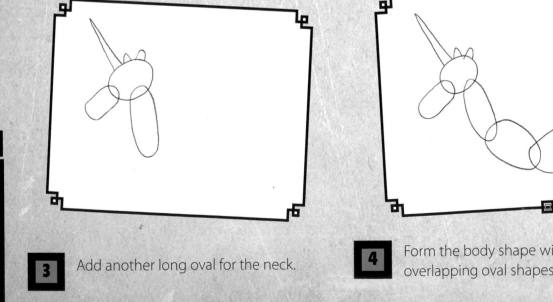

6 Draw thicker lines to connect the oval shapes until you have drawn a clean and more precise unicorn shape. Then erase any lines you don't need.

5 Continue adding oval shapes to form the legs in the position you want them to be to complete the body outline.

7 Add details such as the mane and tail. Add ridges to the unicorn's horn to complete the drawing.

8 To finish this unicorn, color the drawing. If you wish, cut it out and glue the drawing on a background image showing a mythical forest.

DREAMY UNICORN

1 Start with a circle shape for the head. Then add an overlapping oval shape for the body.

2 To complete the outline, add ovals for legs, and a curved shape for the tail.

3 Next, make the tail thicker and fluffier.

4 Follow the shapes and draw a clean outline for your unicorn's body. Erase the guidelines.

5 Outline the mane, then add an ear and the horn. Use curved lines to draw the hoofs.

6 Add details to the mane and the ear. Then draw a dreamy face with just three curved lines. Add two circle shapes for nostrils.

7 Add more details such as the eyelashes. Add ridges to the unicorn's horn to complete the drawing.

8 To finish this dreamy unicorn, color the drawing.

CUTE UNICORN

1 Start with a circle shape for the head. Add an overlapping circle shape for the muzzle. Then form the rest of the body by adding overlapping oval shapes.

2 Next, add more oval shapes to outline the legs.

3 Start outlining the shape of the body. Draw the legs first. Erase the guidelines.

4 Next, follow the shapes and draw a clean outline for the body. Erase the guidelines and draw an S-shaped line for the tail.

5 Outline the mane, then add the ears and the horn. Next, make the tail thicker and fluffier.

6 Clean up the drawing by erasing the guidelines. Then draw the eye and the mouth with just two simple, curved lines. Add two circle shapes for nostrils.

7 Add details such as the eyelashes. Add ridges to the unicorn's horn and a few more lines to the tail to complete the drawing.

8 Color the drawing to finish your project.

UNICORN PORTRAIT

1 Start with an oval shape for the head. Then form the rest of the outline by adding overlapping oval shapes.

2 Add guidelines to the face to outline the features. Add oval shapes to outline the cheek and the muzzle positions.

3 Keep working on the head. Add a triangular shape for the horn and two circles for the nostrils.

4 Draw thicker lines connecting the oval shapes until you have drawn a clean and more precise unicorn shape. Then erase any lines you don't need.

5 Draw the eyes and add details to the nose and the mouth.

6 Next, draw an outline for the mane and the ears. Once you're done, start adding details to the horn.

7 Draw several curved lines to add details to the mane. Add ridges to the unicorn's horn.

8 To finish this proud unicorn portrait, color your art.

DANCING UNICORN

1 Outline the body's position by drawing three circle shapes. Then add one circle shape for the muzzle. Draw two curved lines to mark the angles for the neck and the body.

2 Connect the shapes with curved lines to outline the body. Add another curved line for the tail.

3 Add lines for the legs, and draw small circles to show the joints. Add four rectangular shapes to outline the hoofs.

4 Next, outline the mane. Then add a straight line for the horn position. Add lines to make the tail thicker and fluffier.

5 Follow the shapes and draw a clean outline. Clean up the final outline by erasing any lines you don't need.

6 Draw the eye and the mouth with just two simple curved lines. Add a small oval shape for the nostril. Draw several curved lines to add details to the mane and the tail.

7 Fill in the details. Draw small curved lines to show the muscles. Add ridges to the unicorn's horn and some grass at the unicorn's feet.

8 Color the drawing to finish your project.

CURIOUS UNICORN

1 Start with an oval shape for the head. Then form the rest of the outline by adding overlapping oval shapes.

2 Add a triangular shape to outline the unicorn's horn. Then add oval shapes to the head to outline the positions for the cheek, the eye, and the muzzle.

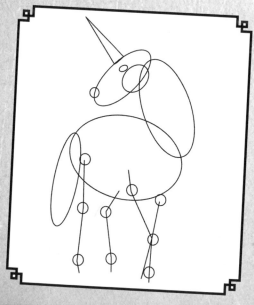

3 Add the lines for the legs and small circles to show the joints.

4 Start filling in the outline for the legs by following the lines.

5 Draw thicker lines connecting the oval shapes until you have drawn a clean and more precise unicorn shape. Then erase any lines you don't need.

6 Next, add details to the tail and draw a thick mane using curved lines. Then draw an eye and nostril.

7 Add details to the mane and to the tail by drawing more curved lines. Add ridges to the unicorn's horn to complete the drawing.

8 Color the drawing to finish your art.

WINGED UNICORN

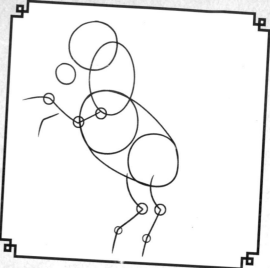

1 Start with a circle shape for the head. Add an overlapping circle shape for the muzzle. Then form the rest of the body by adding overlapping oval shapes.

2 Add lines for the legs, and draw small circles to show the joints.

3 Connect the shapes with curved lines to outline the body. Add another curved line for the tail.

4 Next, follow the shapes and draw the outline for the body. Add a petal shape for the wings and a triangular shape for the horn.

5 Draw thicker lines until you have drawn a clean and more precise unicorn shape. Then erase any lines you don't need.

6 Draw a large manga-style eye and add a simple, curved line for the mouth. Add two small oval shapes for the nostrils.

7 Add details to the eye and ears. Draw hoofs and add ridges to the unicorn's horn. Decorate the body with stars and the wings with an oval-shaped pattern to complete the drawing.

8 To finish this special unicorn, color the drawing.

RESTING UNICORN

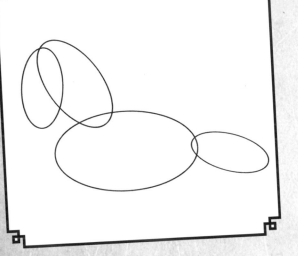

1 Start with an oval shape for the head. Then form the rest of the outline using overlapping oval shapes.

2 Add a triangular shape to outline the unicorn's horn. Then add oval shapes to the head to outline the positions for the cheek, the eye, and the muzzle.

3 Add lines for the legs, and draw small circles to show the joints.

4 Follow the shapes and lines and draw a clean outline for the legs and the body.

5 Draw thicker lines until you have drawn a clean and more precise unicorn shape. Add ears. Then erase any lines you don't need.

6 Next, outline the mane drawing several curved lines.

7 Outline and add curved lines to the tail and draw the hoofs. Draw a big, manga-style eye, add the nostril, and draw ridges for the horn to complete the drawing.

8 Color the drawing to finish your art project.

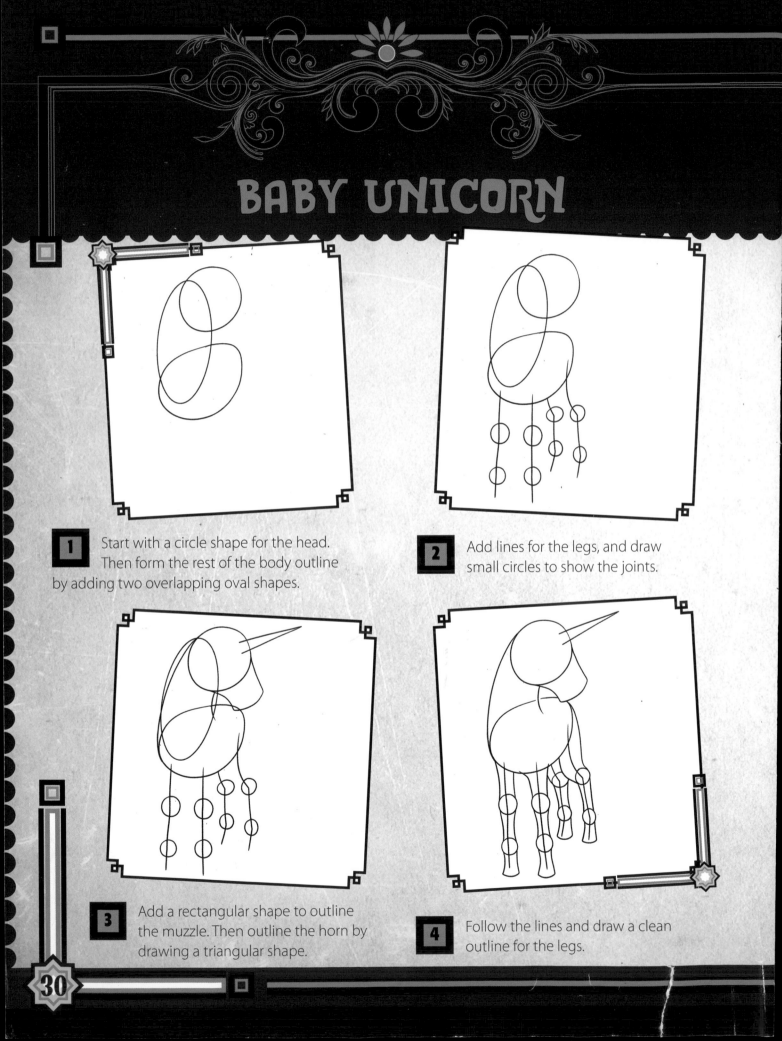

BABY UNICORN

1 Start with a circle shape for the head. Then form the rest of the body outline by adding two overlapping oval shapes.

2 Add lines for the legs, and draw small circles to show the joints.

3 Add a rectangular shape to outline the muzzle. Then outline the horn by drawing a triangular shape.

4 Follow the lines and draw a clean outline for the legs.

5 Next, follow the shapes and draw a clean outline for the body. Erase the guidelines and draw an S-shaped line for the tail.

6 Outline the mane by drawing several curved lines. Add ears and draw a big manga-style eye. Then draw the mouth and nostrils with simple curved lines. Next, make the tail thicker and fluffier.

7 Add details to the eye, then add ridges to the unicorn's horn. Draw the harness, and add the hoofs. Add details to the tail by drawing more curved lines to complete your drawing.

8 To finish this baby unicorn, color the drawing.

GLOSSARY

experimentation Testing to see how well something works.

invaluable Extremely useful.

muzzle The snout of an animal, consisting of the jaws and nose.

palette A board used to mix colors when painting.

pastel A soft and delicate shade of color.

photorealism A style of art that is realistic like a photograph.

spiralled Curled around a central point.

static Does not change.

stubble A very short beard.

texture The feel or appearance of a surface.

FOR MORE INFORMATION

FURTHER READING

James, Elizabeth. *How To Draw for Kids.*
London, UK: Kyle Craig Publishing Ltd., 2016.

Legendre, Philippe. *I Can Draw Animals Around the World.*
Minneapolis, MN: Lerner Publications, 2015.

Sautter, A. J. *How to Draw Griffins, Unicorns, and Other Mythical Beasts.*
North Mankato, MN: Capstone Press, 2016.

WEBSITES

PowerKids Press has developed an online list of websites related to the subject of this book. This site is updated regularly. Please use this link to access the list:
www.powerkidslinks.com/icd/unicorns

INDEX